Animals and US

FUSION

SUPPORT Animals

By E. C. Andrews

BEARPORT PUBLISHING

Minneapolis, Minnesota

Credits
All images are courtesy of Shutterstock.com, unless otherwise specified. With thanks to Getty Images, Thinkstock Photo, and iStockphoto. Recurring – Viktoriia Ablohina. Cover – hchavda. TOC – Maria. 4–5 – River Roaming, Yavdat. 6–7 – Cristina Conti, BetterPhoto. 8–9 – YAKOBCHUK VIACHESLAV, ESB Professional. 10–11 – Tomsickova Tatyana, kobkik, Lysikova Irina. 12–13 – Kolomiyets Viktoriya, myboys.me. 14–15 – Stephen Denness, Santhosh Varghese, bazilfoto. 16–17 – Anton Watman, Irinapsl, Luvtinytoes. 18–19 – A3pfamily, Ben-Schonewille. 20–21 – Milosz_G, Caterina Trimarchi. 22–23 – ANURAK PONGPATIMET, LightField Studio.old

Bearport Publishing Company Product Development Team
Publisher: Jen Jenson; Director of Product Development: Spencer Brinker; Managing Editor: Allison Juda; Editor: Cole Nelson; Associate Editor: Naomi Reich; Associate Editor: Tiana Tran; Art Director: Colin O'Dea; Designer: Kim Jones; Designer: Kayla Eggert; Product Development Specialist: Owen Hamlin

Library of Congress Cataloging-in-Publication Data is available at www.loc.gov or upon request from the publisher.

ISBN: 979-8-89232-732-9 (hardcover)
ISBN: 979-8-89232-782-4 (paperback)
ISBN: 979-8-89232-819-7 (ebook)

For more information, write to Bearport Publishing, 5357 Penn Avenue South, Minneapolis, MN 55419.

Contents

WHAT ARE Support Animals?

Doctors can help people get support animals.

Animals help us in a lot of ways. Some of them help people deal with big feelings. These are called **emotional** (i-MOH-shuh-nuhl) support animals.

Sometimes, feelings can be hard to control or understand. They may even make it hard to pay attention to anything else. Support animals can help people calm down during those times.

It is okay to have big feelings.

A Special KIND OF Animal

Any **domestic** animal can be an emotional support animal. Whether out in public or at home, the animal needs to be very well behaved.

Support animals are not the same as service animals. This is because support animals do not need special training.

These helpful animals are friendly and social. They are comfortable being around people and are happy to spend most of their time with their owners.

WHO NEEDS Support Animals?

Looking after mental health is just as important as looking after the rest of your health.

Mental health has to do with how people feel and think. Sometimes, people may need extra help with their emotions. These feelings can make it hard to get things done.

When a person starts to have big feelings, their heart may begin racing. They might also have trouble breathing. A support animal can help them calm down.

The friendship between animals and owners helps people feel less lonely.

Dogs

Dogs can have close **bonds** with their owners. This helps a support dog know when their owner is feeling upset or scared. The clever animal may lick their owner's hand to help them **relax**.

Going on walks is often good for a person's mental health.

Good support dogs must listen to their owner's commands. They need to stay calm even in busy or loud places. A support dog can sense how their owner is feeling by looking at their face.

Many types of dogs are easy to train.

Cats

Cats are often quieter than dogs. Most cats are naturally calm. This helps their owners feel calm, too.

Petting cats can help owners feel more at ease.

Good support cats are easy to care for. They are **independent**, so they are comfortable spending time on their own. But these furry friends can be cuddly as well!

Parakeets

Unlike most animals, parakeets can speak human languages! They do this by copying what they hear. Parakeets have loud voices and are often very friendly.

Parakeets can stay calm as they are held or petted by their owner.

These bubbly birds make great support animals for people who cannot move easily or are often inside. Parakeets do not need to be taken out to go to the bathroom like dogs or other animals do.

A Parakeet's claw

A parakeet uses its claws to **perch** on its owner's hand.

Rats

Domestic rats are very social. They enjoy spending time with people. The rats often climb on their owners' hands or shoulders to cuddle.

Rats are small and easy to care for.

Rat owners do not need to bathe these tiny animals. These support animals can clean themselves by rubbing and licking their bodies.

A rat cleaning itself

Since rats are social animals, many people get two or more.

Parrots

Parrots are very loving toward their owners. These clever birds can tell when a person is angry or sad. Parrots do this by watching the way their owners act.

Some parrots can be taught to play fetch!

Parrots live much longer than most other support animals.

Parrots may help people is by learning calming words. When owners are upset, parrots can repeat these words to help them feel better.

Chickens

Chickens can also be support animals! These birds are energetic. Chickens can easily form bonds with people. The clucking noises they make help their owners feel less alone.

A support chicken can be held by their owner.

Unlike some other support animals, chickens can take care of themselves for most of the day. Owners only need to make sure they are fed and kept safe at night.

Chickens usually spend their days pecking for food.

Support Animals AND US

There are many kinds of support animals that help people in different ways. They play an important role in making our lives easier and happier.

Support animals help people with their mental health. Spending time with these animal helpers lets people know they are not alone.

Glossary

bonds close friendships or connections with people

domestic tamed for use by humans

emotional having to do with someone's feelings

independent able to do things without help from someone else

mental health how well we feel in our minds

perch to sit or stand on the edge of something

relax to stop feeling nervous or worried

Index